TALKING BAILS

Also available

The Funniest Football Quotes... Ever!
The Funniest Tennis Quotes... Ever!
The Funniest Liverpool Quotes... Ever!
The Funniest Chelsea Quotes... Ever!
The Funniest West Ham Quotes... Ever!
The Funniest Spurs Quotes... Ever!
The Funniest Arsenal Quotes... Ever!
The Funniest Man City Quotes... Ever!
The Funniest Newcastle Quotes... Ever!
The Funniest United Quotes... Ever!
The Funniest Leeds Quotes... Ever!
The Funniest Boro Quotes... Ever!
The Funniest Forest Quotes... Ever!
The Funniest Sunderland Quotes... Ever!
The Funniest Leicester Quotes... Ever!
The Funniest Saints Quotes... Ever!
The Funniest Everton Quotes... Ever!
The Funniest Villa Quotes... Ever!
The Funniest QPR Quotes... Ever!
The Funniest England Quotes... Ever!

THE FUNNIEST CRICKET QUOTES... EVER!

"That was unplayable, just like the Spice Girls."

"I was so carried away with drink and emotion, I spoke Egyptian."

by Gordon Law

Copyright © 2022 by Eagle Books.

No part of this publication may be reproduced, stored in a retrieval system or transmitted in any form by any means, electronic, mechanical, photocopying, or otherwise, without prior written permission of the publisher Eagle Books.

contact@gmediagroup.co.uk

Printed in Europe and the USA

ISBN: 978-1-917744-20-1
Imprint: Eagle Books

TALKING BAILS

The funniest cricket broadcaster quotes!

TALKING BAILS

"A very small crowd here today. I can count the people on one hand. Can't be more than 30."
Michael Abrahamson

"Strangely, in slow-motion replay, the ball seemed to hang in the air for even longer."
David Acfield

"Owais Shah is about to start coming hard."
Chris Adams

"It's never easy putting a rubber on, is it, Michael?"
Jonathan Agnew to Michael Vaughan

The funniest cricket broadcaster quotes!

"I've never got to the bottom of streaking."

Jonathan Agnew

"He's scored one or two boundaries in his seven."

Jonathan Agnew

"It's a beautiful day today and as I look around the ground I can see about 30 young girls all wearing Dutch caps."

Jonathan Agnew

"Paul Collingwood is proving to be a very good tosser."

Jonathan Agnew

"He didn't quite manage to get his leg over."
Jonathan Agnew, after Ian Botham had spun around off balance and tried to step over the wicket unsuccessfully

"The Zimbabwean fans have been quite quiet; now there are dozens of them starting to expose themselves."
Jonathan Agnew

"Like an elephant trying to do the pole vault."
Jonathan Agnew on Inzamam-ul-Haq after the rotund player fell over his own stumps

The funniest cricket broadcaster quotes!

"I definitely believe if any of our batsmen get out to [Ashley] Giles in the Tests they should go and hang themselves. But I'm confident that won't happen."

Terry Alderman... and it did happen

"Umpire Fenwich just itches his nose, rather than putting his finger up in the usual fashion."

Paul Allott

"On the outfield, hundreds of small boys are playing with their balls."

Rex Alston

TALKING BAILS

"He played a cut so late as to be positively posthumous."
John Arlott

"Bill Frindall has done a bit of mental arithmetic with a calculator."
John Arlott

"The umpire signals a bye with the air of a weary stalk."
John Arlott

"Pietersen's sticky patch was a very small one."
Mike Atherton

The funniest cricket broadcaster quotes!

"Shane Warne turned around like a can of beans."

Mike Atherton

"When you restrict a side to 170, 99 times out of 10 you feel confident."

Mike Atherton

"[Ray Jennings] was to orthodoxy what King Herod was to child-minding."

Mike Atherton on the South African coach

"Unbelievable scenes for Cockermouth Cricket Club, with Hugh Jardon bowling 6 for 9!"

Mike Atherton tricked into reading a rude tweet

TALKING BAILS

"To win a three-match series you really want to be looking at winning two of the matches."
Mike Atherton

"Leaving out Dennis Lillee against England would be as unthinkable as the Huns dropping Attila."
Australian TV commentator

"Well, Andrew Strauss is certainly an optimist – he's come out wearing sunblock."
Australian commentator in the fifth Test of the 2006-07 series whitewash

The funniest cricket broadcaster quotes!

"In Australia we have a word to describe their [Pakistan's] way of playing: laissez-faire."
Aussie commentator

"A wicket could always fall in this game, literally at any time."
Trevor Bailey

"Tavare has literally dropped anchor."
Trevor Bailey

"His tail is literally up!"
Trevor Bailey

TALKING BAILS

"The game minus slow bowling is like bread without butter or, even worse, French cuisine without the sauces."

Trevor Bailey

"The Port Elizabeth ground is more of a circle than an oval. It is long and square."

Trevor Bailey

"He's on 90... 10 away from that mythical figure."

Trevor Bailey

The funniest cricket broadcaster quotes!

"Then there was that dark horse with the golden arm, Mudassar Nazar."

Trevor Bailey

"The obvious successor to Brearly at the moment isn't obvious."

Trevor Bailey

"There are good one-day players, there are good Test players and vice versa."

Trevor Bailey

TALKING BAILS

"Sean Pollock there, a carbon copy of his dad. Except he's a bit taller and he's got red hair."

Trevor Bailey

"The first time you face up to a googly you're going to be in trouble if you've never faced one before."

Trevor Bailey

"It's especially tense for Parker, who's literally fighting for a place on an overcrowded plane to India."

Trevor Bailey

The funniest cricket broadcaster quotes!

"Mudassar has really put the icing on the day for the visitors."

Trevor Bailey

"That's another nail in what looks like being a very good score."

Trevor Bailey

"No captain with all the hindsight in the world can predict how the wicket is going to play."

Trevor Bailey

"Lloyd did what he achieved with that shot."

Trevor Bailey

TALKING BAILS

"This is the sort of pitch which literally castrates a bowler."

Trevor Bailey

"This series has been swings and pendulums all the way through."

Trevor Bailey

"I don't think he expected it, and that's what caught him unawares."

Trevor Bailey

"Logie decided to chance his arm and it came off."

Trevor Bailey

The funniest cricket broadcaster quotes!

"Malcolm Marshall scored a handful of runs at Headingley... nought and one."

Jack Bannister

"And the rest not only is history but will remain history for many years to come."

Jack Bannister

"Zimbabwe have done well, just as it looked as though the horse had left the stable and gone galloping down the road, they managed to put a chain on the door."

Peter Baxter

TALKING BAILS

"Now Ramprakash is facing a fish of a rather different feather in Mark Waugh."

Peter Baxter

"And now an erect MCC member has been sat down... and this slightly sticky period continues."

BBC commentator

"Andrew Flintoff is to see a renowned joint specialist in Amsterdam."

BBC radio sports bulletin

"Yorkshire 332 all out, Hutton ill. Sorry, Hutton 111."

BBC newsreader John Snagge

The funniest cricket broadcaster quotes!

"And this game is coming nicely to a climax; like a well-cooked Welsh rabbit."

BBC commentator

"Courtney Walsh ripped the heart out of England both metaphorically and physically."

BBC commentator

"Whenever they win the toss, for example, South Africa either bat first or field first."

Tony Becca

"He's nearly 34 – in fact he's 33."

Richie Benaud

TALKING BAILS

"There were no scores below single figures."

Richie Benaud

"That slow-motion replay doesn't show how fast the ball was travelling."

Richie Benaud

"There were congratulations and high sixes all round."

Richie Benaud

"He's usually a good puller, but that time he couldn't get it up."

Richie Benaud

The funniest cricket broadcaster quotes!

"I think the batsman's strategy will be to make runs and not get out."
Richie Benaud

"The only possible result is a draw. The alternative is a win for England."
Richie Benaud

"Even Downton couldn't get down high enough for that."
Richie Benaud

"There are a lot of hookers around the world."
Richie Benaud

TALKING BAILS

"And Glenn McGrath dismissed for two, just 98 runs short of his century."

Richie Benaud

"There was a slight interruption for the athletics."

Richie Benaud on a streaker

"And for Fidel Castro, there's an extra man placed on the midwicket boundary."

Richie Benaud actually meant Fidel Edwards

"Laird has been brought in to stand in the corner of the circle."

Richie Benaud

The funniest cricket broadcaster quotes!

"Gatting at fine leg – that's a contradiction in terms."

Richie Benaud

"The hallmark of a great captain is the ability to win the toss at the right time."

Richie Benaud

"His throw went absolutely nowhere near where it was going."

Richie Benaud

"This shirt is unique, there are only 200 of them."

Richie Benaud

"Captaincy is 90 per cent luck and 10 per cent skill. But don't try it without that 10 per cent."
Richie Benaud

"Because out in the field, you haven't got anyone whispering into your ear saying all sorts of things, you've got to do it yourself."
Richie Benaud

"Don't bother looking for that, let alone chasing it. That's gone straight into the confectionery stall and out again."
Richie Benaud

The funniest cricket broadcaster quotes!

"The spectators are jumping around like dervishes at a teddy bears' picnic."

Richie Benaud

"He's not quite got hold of that one. If he had, it would have gone for nine."

Richie Benaud on a Justin Langer six

"It's been a very slow and dull day, but it hasn't been boring. It's been a good, entertaining day's cricket."

Tony Benneworth, ABC Radio

TALKING BAILS

"They've sent Shah in at three. It's a good move, it'll give him time to play himself in before he explodes."
Harsha Bhogle

"In Hampshire's innings the Smith brothers scored 13 and 52 respectively."
Henry Blofeld

"The lights are shining quite darkly."
Henry Blofeld

"Klusener holds that bat like a piece of wood."
Henry Blofeld

The funniest cricket broadcaster quotes!

Henry Blofeld: "You'd want Geoffrey Boycott to bat for your life."

Alec Stewart: "It would either be a long life or a slow death."

"In the rear, the small diminutive figure of Shoaib Mohammad, who can't be much taller than he is."

Henry Blofeld

"Oh, and here comes Caddick to bowl from the pavilion end again – well, I don't suppose he'll mind if I read the scores between his balls."

Henry Blofeld

TALKING BAILS

"Their heads were on their chins."

Henry Blofeld

"We had a winking seagull the other day. You don't often see a seagull wink."

Henry Blofeld

"Brian Toss won the close."

Henry Blofeld

"If the tension here was a block of Cheddar cheese, you could cut it with a knife."

Henry Blofeld

The funniest cricket broadcaster quotes!

"It's a catch he would have caught 99 times out of 1,000."
Henry Blofeld

"He is like a guardsman; every part of him erect."
Henry Blofeld

"Kevin Pietersen looks like a meerkat."
Ravi Bopara

"Stuart Broad reminds me of a woman."
Ravi Bopara

"After their 60 overs, West Indies have scored 244 for 7, all out."

Frank Bough

"A few years ago England would have struggled to beat the Eskimos."

Ian Botham

"At the end of the day, it's September."

Ian Botham

"England need to pick players who do not have skeletons in their coffins."

Ian Botham

The funniest cricket broadcaster quotes!

"I am colour-blind, which makes me worry about what clothes I put on in the morning. My wife matches my shirts and ties in advance."
Ian Botham

Ian Botham: "Where were you last night?"
David Lloyd: "An oyster bar – apparently it puts lead in your pencil. I don't know about that. I think it only matters if you have got someone to write to."

"I go in planes and helicopters because they're meant to fly. Commentary boxes aren't."
Ian Botham on refusing to climb so high up

"I feel so bad about my OBE I'm going to tie it round my cat. It doesn't mean anything anymore. It's a joke."

Geoffrey Boycott after England's cricketers were given MBEs

"They should cut Joel Garner off at the knees to make him bowl at normal height."

Geoffrey Boycott

"Are you taught to talk PR, because I'm sick of hearing it. Why doesn't someone put their hand up and say, 'We played rubbish'?"

Geoffrey Boycott to Stuart Broad

The funniest cricket broadcaster quotes!

"Paul Harris is a buffet bowler – you just help yourself."

Geoffrey Boycott

"You've got to make split-second decisions so quickly."

Geoffrey Boycott

"I'm glad two sides of the cherry have been put forward."

Geoffrey Boycott

"As the ball gets softer it loses its hardness."

Geoffrey Boycott

"Hauritz doesn't look like he could bowl my mum out, then he gets our best batsman out."

Geoffrey Boycott

"He could have caught that between the cheeks of his backside."

Geoffrey Boycott

"England have a very English attack."

Geoffrey Boycott

"To stay in, you've got to not get out."

Geoffrey Boycott

The funniest cricket broadcaster quotes!

"If I was on 99 and at the other end and you got out, I'd hit you with my bat."

Geoffrey Boycott to Matthew Hoggard

"I reckon my mum could have caught that in her pinny!"

Geoffrey Boycott

"More brains in a pork pie."

Geoffrey Boycott on Kevin Pietersen

"I'll cross that chestnut when we get to it."

Geoffrey Boycott

TALKING BAILS

"If England lose now, they will be leaving the field with their heads between their legs."
Geoffrey Boycott

"It would be unprintable on television."
Geoffrey Boycott

"If my mum was alive she could captain England to play West Indies... hopeless, aren't they?"
Geoffrey Boycott

"Fortunately it was a slow ball, so it wasn't a fast one."
Geoffrey Boycott

The funniest cricket broadcaster quotes!

"Such an easy pitch... Graham Gooch and Alec Stewart think their Christmases have all come home."

Geoffrey Boycott

"Glen McGrath bowled so badly in his first Test as though he'd never bowled in a Test match before."

Geoffrey Boycott

"He was the England cricket coach, but he always had a face like thunder. He gave the impression he was walking around with piles."

Geoffrey Boycott on Duncan Fletcher

TALKING BAILS

"How do you get bowled out in 32 overs? I would have just been getting my eye in."
Geoffrey Boycott on England's Ashes squad

TalkSport's Alan Brazil: "Do you know if Hansie Cronje is doing any media work during the cricket World Cup?"
Cricket expert: "Well, that'd be a bit hard from beyond the grave, mate."

"Alderman knows that he's either going to get a wicket, or he isn't."
Steve Brenkley

The funniest cricket broadcaster quotes!

"You almost run out of expletives for this man's fielding."
Chris Broad

"Merv Hughes always appeared to be wearing a tumble-dried ferret on his top lip."
Rick Broadbent

"The other advantage England have got when Phil Tufnell is bowling is that he isn't fielding."
Ian Chappell

"It's tough for a natural hooker to give it up."
Ian Chappell

TALKING BAILS

"Fast bowlers are quick, even at the end of the day. Just watch this – admittedly it's in slow motion."

Ian Chappell

"I would rather I never have to see him again but unfortunately we work fairly close together."

Ian Chappell on Ian Botham

"Not sure the ladies will appreciate their age being put up there."

Ian Chappell gives a piece of advice to the TV networks while watching the Women's T20 World Cup

The funniest cricket broadcaster quotes!

"To dismiss this lad [Mike] Denness you don't have to bowl fast, you just have to run up fast."

Brian Close

"Three bad days does not mean you're a bad team overnight."

Paul Collingwood

"It's been hard to penetrate their batsmen."

Paul Collingwood

"The Test Match begins in 10 minutes – that's our time, of course."

David Coleman

TALKING BAILS

"That was a sort of parson's nose innings – good in parts."

Charles Colville

"Harmison likes to play every shot in the book, sometimes to the same ball."

Charles Colville

"Well, Pietersen wasn't even into double figures, he'd only scored 15."

Charles Colville

The funniest cricket broadcaster quotes!

"Trying to get a ball past him is like trying to sneak a sunrise past a rooster."

Jeremy Coney on bowling to Brian Lara

"Skipper Moin Khan has really earned his socks out there today."

Chris Cowdrey

"The Queen's Park Oval – as its name suggests, absolutely round!"

Tony Cozier

TALKING BAILS

"England have their noses in front, not only actually, but metaphorically too."

Tony Cozier

"Now Botham, with a chance to put everything that's gone before behind him."

Tony Cozier

"Angus Fraser's bowling is like shooting down F16 aeroplanes with sling shots. Even if they hit, no damage would be done. Like an old horse, he should be put out to pasture."

Colin Croft

The funniest cricket broadcaster quotes!

"The only person who could be better than Brian Lara is Brian Lara himself."
Colin Croft

"The ball came back, literally cutting Graham Thorpe in half."
Colin Croft

"Mike Atherton's a thinking captain: he gives the impression of someone with his head on all the time."
Colin Croft

TALKING BAILS

"Pakistan always have the same problem – too many chiefs and not enough Indians."

Robert Croft

"England were beaten in the sense that they lost."

Dickie Davis

"David Boon is now completely clean-shaven, except for his moustache."

Graham Dawson

The funniest cricket broadcaster quotes!

"That's a remarkable catch by Yardley, especially as the ball quite literally rolled along the ground towards him."

Mike Denness

"The last rites are on the wall here."

Allan Donald

"It's difficult being more laid back than David Gower without actually being comatose."

Frances Edmonds

"Pakistan can play well, but they have the ability to play badly, too."

John Emburey

"This game was another rung on the ladder of the learning curve."

John Emburey

"Sunny, don't get out first ball – it's a long way back to the pavilion."

Farokh Engineer... before the player was given out first ball

The funniest cricket broadcaster quotes!

"If Gower hadn't caught that, it would have decapitated his hand."

Farokh Engineer

"There must be something on Gooch's mind and he wants to get it off his chest."

Farokh Engineer

"This MCG wicket has more bounce than a Baywatch beach sprint."

Damien Fleming on the spring in the Melbourne wicket

TALKING BAILS

"The Sri Lankan team have lost their heads – literally."

Gemini Ganesan

"With global warming, the sun is a lot stronger nowadays."

Sunil Gavaskar on an increasing number of drinks breaks

"Glenn McGrath joins Craig McDermott and Paul Reiffel in a three-ponged prace attack."

Tim Gavel, ABC News

The funniest cricket broadcaster quotes!

"This is Cunis at the Vauxhall End. Cunis – a funny sort of name. Neither one thing or the other."

Alan Gibson

"How can you have a clash of cultures when you're playing against a country with no culture?"

David Gower ahead of the Ashes

"Once again our consistency has been proved to be inconsistent."

David Graveney

TALKING BAILS

"Yes, he's a very good cricketer – pity he's not a better batter or bowler."

Tom Graveney

"In the back of Hughes' mind must be the thought that he will dance down the piss and mitch one."

Tony Greig

"The Aussies try to present a tough-guy image, but this present generation are a bunch of cissies."

Tony Greig

The funniest cricket broadcaster quotes!

"For every winner, there has to be a loser in these games."

Tony Greig

"Marshall's bowling with his head."

Tony Greig

"Clearly the West Indies are going to play their normal game, which is what they normally do."

Tony Greig

"David Lloyd is speaking to his slippers."

Tony Greig

TALKING BAILS

"This run of 24 games without defeat must be like a millstone on your shoulders."

Tony Gubba

"Being the manager of a touring team is rather like being in charge of a cemetery – lots of people underneath you, but no one listening."

West Indies' Wes Hall

"He reminds me of a newly-born giraffe."

Matthew Hayden after Ishant Sharma slipped during his run-up

The funniest cricket broadcaster quotes!

"Ashley Giles made a simple attempt at a top-edged hook by Mahela Jayawardene look like a Mr Bean Christmas special."
Peter Hayter

"At least when Zimbabwe beat us in '83 we were drinking cans the night before. And lots of them."
Rodney Hogg after the Aussies' defeat

"In my playing days the ice was kept for the beers."
Michael Holding on the modern routines

TALKING BAILS

"Hopefully you won't be calling me Bish."
Michael Holding to Virat Kohli – he was twice called "Bish" by Faf du Plessis at the toss

"Anderson, give him a coconut, he'll swing it."
Michael Holding on James Anderson

"In most cricketing dismissals there's usually a human element involved."
Michael Holding

"The most important thing about batting is getting the bat to hit the ball."
Michael Holding

The funniest cricket broadcaster quotes!

"The one thing Australian batsmen don't like is those dibbly dobbers."

Michael Holding

"It's obviously a great occasion for all the players. It's a moment they will always forget."

Ray Hudson

"Look at [Jamie] Siddons. He's ready to throw like a panther."

Kim Hughes

"Other than mistakes, he hasn't put a foot wrong."

Simon Hughes

TALKING BAILS

"The great thing about Stuart Broad is that his length probes relentlessly."

Simon Hughes

"The sight of Imran [Khan] tearing fearsomely down the hill and the baying of the crowd made me realise for the first time that adrenalin was sometimes brown."

Simon Hughes

"Devon Smith looks like the sort of guy you can imagine pumping himself."

Nasser Hussain

The funniest cricket broadcaster quotes!

"Jimmy Anderson will have to get his length right when he faces Butt."

Nasser Hussain

"Ponting will be thinking, we dished up filth."

Nasser Hussain

"Stuart Broad is putting it in the batsman's slot."

Nasser Hussain

"He's got his hands up in the middle of his arms."

Nasser Hussain

"There's a concern for cricket because the goal posts are moving."

Nasser Hussain

"Michael Clarke desperately wants a couple of extra inches."

Nasser Hussain

"He stood on tiptoe, on the back foot, and drove the ball on the off. I don't quite know how you'd describe that shot."

Ray Illingworth

The funniest cricket broadcaster quotes!

"He didn't drop the bat. It fell out of his hand."

Ray Illingworth

"Pollock is such a good bowler, it hasn't even taken him a single delivery to get it on the spot."

Robin Jackman

"He seems to have had a problem with his right foot, which has run with him all day."

Robin Jackman

"Fourteen overs left, that's seven from each end."

Robin Jackman

TALKING BAILS

"Sachin Tendulkar is a great cricketer but he walks and goes to the toilet like all of us."
Ray Jennings

"The team that doesn't win will find itself on the losing side."
Neil Johnson

"And now it's over to Rex Alston for some balls."
Brian Johnston

"And that's Dickie Bird standing there with his neck between his shoulders."
Brian Johnston

The funniest cricket broadcaster quotes!

"As he comes in to bowl, Freddie Titmus has got two short legs, one of them square."

Brian Johnston

"Butcher plays this off the black foot."

Brian Johnston

"Henry Horton's got a funny stance. It looks as if he's shitting on a shooting stick."

Brian Johnston

"He used to work for a very well-known firm – can't remember who they are."

Brian Johnston

TALKING BAILS

"This bowler's like my dog: three short legs and balls which swing each way."

Brian Johnston

"Ray Illingworth has just relieved himself at the Pavilion End."

Brian Johnston

"Well, I shall remember that catch for many a dying day."

Brian Johnston

"And a sedentary seagull flies by."

Brian Johnston

The funniest cricket broadcaster quotes!

"Ah yes, sledging. In the days before microphones on the pitch, we got that blind MP chap up into the commentary box to lip read."

Brian Johnston

"There's Neil Harvey standing at leg slip with his legs wide apart, waiting for a tickle."

Brian Johnston

"We welcome World Service listeners to the Oval, where the bowler's Holding, the batsman's Willey."

Brian Johnston

TALKING BAILS

"I don't think I have ever seen anything quite like that before – it's the second time it's happened today."
Brian Johnston

"Massif Arsood."
Brian Johnston means Asif Masood

"One ball left."
Brian Johnston as Glenn Turner went back to bat after being hit in the groin area

"There's a dirty black crowd here."
Brian Johnston referring to a rain cloud

The funniest cricket broadcaster quotes!

"Greg Chappell instructed his brother Trevor to bowl the last ball underground."

Richard Kaufman

"That's the second time Maher has been bitten – beaten."

Rod Kilner

"An interesting morning, full of interest."

Jim Laker

"It's a unique occasion really – a repeat of Melbourne 1977."

Jim Laker

TALKING BAILS

"England have no McGrathish bowlers. There are hardly any McGrathish bowlers, except for [Glenn] McGrath."
Stuart Law

"There's nothing like the sound of flesh on leather to get a cricket match going."
Geoff Lawson

"It was all so easy for Walsh. All he had to do was drop an arm and there it was, on the ground."
Tony Lewis

The funniest cricket broadcaster quotes!

"Jon Lewis is a real Essex boy… born in Isleworth, Middlesex."

Tony Lewis

"Aussie twelfth man Ronald McDonald brought on a triple burger with relish. But England need a large Scotch!"

David Lloyd

"What do I think of the reverse sweep? It's like Manchester United getting a penalty and Bryan Robson taking it with his head."

David Lloyd

TALKING BAILS

"If he [Paul Collingwood] was playing outside your house, you'd shut the curtains."

David Lloyd

"Graeme Smith showed us how big he can get."

David Lloyd

"We've had the main course and now it's time for the hors d'oeuvres and cheese."

David Lloyd

"He is a very dangerous bowler. Innocuous, if you like."

David Lloyd on Chris Harris

The funniest cricket broadcaster quotes!

"England have nothing to lose here, apart from this Test match."

David Lloyd

"They've got to swing like a 70s disco to get anywhere near from here."

David Lloyd

"In the circumstances, I felt I should oblige. She was a lovely mature lady, and quite ample. In fact, Muttiah Muralitharan would have had plenty of room to sign his name."

David Lloyd when a former ladies cricketer asked him to sign her cleavage with a felt-tip pen for charity

TALKING BAILS

"You won't get me knocking him as a cricketer, but as a man I detest him."

David Lloyd on Geoffrey Boycott

"It's like a benefit match, is this. There'll be someone going round with a raffle before long."

David Lloyd on the Bangladesh attack

"If this bloke's a Test Match bowler, then my backside is a fire engine."

David Lloyd on Nathan Astle

"Hook, line and Sinclair."

David Lloyd on Mathew Sinclair getting out

The funniest cricket broadcaster quotes!

"You can't get out any earlier than the second ball of the game."

David Lloyd

"Is that Ranatunga? Strewth, he's not missed many lunches has he?"

David Lloyd on a rather large looking Arjuna Ranatunga watching in the stands at Kandy

"Imagine if you got him on a triple word score in Scrabble."

David Lloyd on Chaminda Vaas' five first names

TALKING BAILS

"Ricky Ponting looks like how I would imagine Jimmy Krankie would've turned out with the aid of human growth hormones."
Gabby Logan

"England might now be the favourites to draw this match."
Vic Marks

"His back injury is behind him."
Christopher Martin-Jenkins

"He's got two short legs breathing down his neck."
Christopher Martin-Jenkins

The funniest cricket broadcaster quotes!

"And we don't need a calculator to tell us that the run-rate required is 4.5454 per over."

Christopher Martin-Jenkins

"And Marshall throws his head to his hands."

Christopher Martin-Jenkins

"It's a perfect day here in Australia, glorious blue sunshine."

Christopher Martin-Jenkins

"And you can't ignore what's going on under the water of the iceberg either."

Christopher Martin-Jenkins

TALKING BAILS

"It's his second finger – technically his third."

Christopher Martin-Jenkins

"It is now possible they can get the impossible score they first thought possible."

Christopher Martin-Jenkins

"Gul has another ball in his hand and bowls to Bell, who has two."

Christopher-Martin Jenkins

"If you go in with two fast bowlers and one breaks down, you're left two short."

Bob Massie, ABC Radio

The funniest cricket broadcaster quotes!

"It was only a brief shower, well it was briefer than that."

Jim Maxwell

"This game will be over anytime from now."

Alan McGilvray

"He only came unstuck against the ball that bowled him."

Simon Metcalf

"I've seen batting all over the world. And in other countries too."

Keith Miller

TALKING BAILS

"Where's your hanky, love?"

Danny Morrison to a tearful RCB supporter

"Boycott, somewhat a creature of habit, likes exactly the sort of food he himself prefers."

Dan Mosey

"He'll certainly want to start by getting off the mark."

Dan Mosey

"Well, everyone is enjoying this except Vic Marks, and I think he's enjoying himself."

Dan Mosey

The funniest cricket broadcaster quotes!

"Dean Headly has left the field with a back injury... more news on that as soon as it breaks."
Pat Murphy

"And he's got the guts to score runs when the crunch is down."
John Murray

"One of the girls has been fingered by officials."
New Zealand commentator

"Michael Vaughan has a long history in the game ahead of him."
Mark Nicholas

TALKING BAILS

"It's now 2-0 to England with two to play – and they're both to come."

Mark Nicholas

"It's cricket porn when he blocks it."

Kerry O'Keeffe on Kane Williamson's batting

"The stumps have asked for pads."

Kerry O'Keeffe on Rahul Dravid who had been bowled six times in seven innings

"Andre Nel is big and raw-boned and I suspect he has the IQ of an empty swimming pool."

Adam Parore

The funniest cricket broadcaster quotes!

"It's only a matter of time before the end of his innings."

Michael Peschardt

"And as so often with the Achilles tendon injuries, the Achilles goes."

Pat Pocock

"It was close for Zaheer, Lawson threw his hands in the air and Marsh threw his head in the air."

Jack Potter

"Alan Kourie looks calm, but inside his chest beats a heart."
Trevor Quirk

"And there's the George Headley Stand, named after George Headley."
Trevor Quirk

"There's only one man made more appeals than you, George, and that was Dr Barnardo."
Bill Reeve to Yorkshire and England's George Macaulay

The funniest cricket broadcaster quotes!

"Border was facing a four-paced prong attack."

Dave Renneberg, ABC Radio

"The only time an Australian walks is when his car runs out of petrol."

Barry Richards

"He's 99.6 per cent perfect."

Viv Richards on Sachin Tendulkar

"It's a very good witch in Bombay... good wicket."

Greg Ritchie

TALKING BAILS

"Border is a walnut: hard to crack and without much to please the eye."

Peter Roebuck

"This ground is surprising. It holds about 60,000 but when there are around 30,000 in, you get the feeling that it is half empty."

Ravi Shastri

"By the time he picks up his broom, the sh*t has hit the ceiling."

Ravi Shastri describes MS Dhoni batting down the lower order

The funniest cricket broadcaster quotes!

"The crowd realises there's a match on here."

Ravi Shastri

"I'll have no job left if the toss is done away with."

Ravi Shastri

"That was intentional from Gambhir."

Ravi Shastri as Gautam Gambhir hits a four

"A brain scan revealed that Andrew Caddick is not suffering from a fracture of the shin."

Jo Sheldon

TALKING BAILS

"He played that like a dwarf at a urinal."

Navjot Sidhu as Sachin Tendulkar stood on his toes to play the ball

"Umpire Eddie Nichols is a man who cannot find his own buttocks with his two hands."

Navjot Sidhu

"The third umpires should be changed as often as nappies... and for the same reason."

Navjot Sidhu

"With his lovely soft hands he just tossed it off."

Bobby Simpson

The funniest cricket broadcaster quotes!

"It's a difficult catch to take, especially when you're running away from the ball."
Sky Sports commentator

"Some say he's 45, but after that I'd say he's 32."
Michael Slater is impressed by (the 38-year-old) Shahid Afridi's one-handed catch

"Does David Warner have any weaknesses in HD?"
Ian Smith promotes Channel 9's high definition coverage

TALKING BAILS

"England have played pretty well – just their cricket let them down."

Ian Smith

"Ricky Martin."

Kris Srikkanth means Ricky Ponting

"England players traditionally have been playing very traditional cricket."

Kris Srikkanth

"If Srinath can bowl a little extra pace, it will make the ball come to the bat more faster."

Kris Srikkanth

The funniest cricket broadcaster quotes!

"England players have a typical English-like attitude, which is different than Pakistani attitude."

Kris Srikkanth

"Chris Lewis didn't bowl, then came in and scored 30. A top all-round effort."

Alec Stewart

"The dew in India is really wet."

Scott Styris

"I'd have looked even faster in colour."

Fred Trueman

TALKING BAILS

"England's always expecting. No wonder they call her the Mother Country."

Fred Trueman

"Anyone foolish enough to predict the outcome of this match is a fool."

Fred Trueman

"Unless something happens that we can't predict, I don't think a lot will happen."

Fred Trueman

The funniest cricket broadcaster quotes!

"There's only one head bigger than Tony Greig's and that's Birkenhead."

Fred Trueman

"Unless somebody can pull a miracle out of the fire, Somerset are cruising into the semi-final."

Fred Trueman

"I'm not one to blame anyone, but it was definitely Viv Richards' fault."

Fred Trueman

TALKING BAILS

"If Boycott played cricket the way he talked, he would have had people queuing up to get into the ground instead of queuing up to leave."

Fred Trueman

"That's what cricket is all about, two batsmen pitting their wits against one another."

Fred Trueman

"That was a tremendous six – the ball was still in the air as it went over the boundary."

Fred Trueman

The funniest cricket broadcaster quotes!

"If there is a game that attracts the half-baked theorists more than cricket, I have yet to hear of it."

Fred Trueman

"The crowd is flocking into the ground slowly."

Frank Tyson

"It is important for Pakistan to take wickets if they are going to make inroads into this Australian batting line-up."

Max Walker

TALKING BAILS

"One day there will be radio with pictures."
Max Walker

"Hardie was a solid rock upon which Essex hung their caps."
Peter Walker

"He has got perfect control over the ball right up to the minute he lets it go."
Peter Walker

"The England women's cricket team are such an outstanding crack unit."
Ian Ward

The funniest cricket broadcaster quotes!

"Denis Compton was the only player to call his partner for a run and wish him good luck at the same time."

John Warr

"And we have just heard, although this is not the latest score from Bournemouth, that Hampshire have beaten Nottinghamshire by nine wickets."

Peter West

"Pietersen's just stroked Vettori through the covers."

Arlo White

"I have seen fewer hookers in Soho on a Saturday night."

Bob Willis on England's struggles with the short ball against India

"When there's a hosepipe ban covering three-quarters of the country, you don't expect a damp wicket at Lord's."

Bob Willis

"If that'd been a hamburger he'd have stopped it."

Bob Willis has a swipe at a portly Ian Blackwell during a misfield

The funniest cricket broadcaster quotes!

"He's taking the bull by the horns here, and throwing everything at it."

Bob Willis

"Australia must now climb to the top diving board for a last desperate throw of the dice."

Bob Willis

"The Aussie all-rounder Andrew McDonald is more like Ronald McDonald."

Bob Willis

"This really is a fairy-book start."

Bob Willis

TALKING BAILS

"Vengsarkar taking a simple catch at square leg, the ball literally dropping down his throat."

Bob Willis

"Daryl Harper, hopeless. Billy Bowden, a show-pony. Steve Bucknor, past his sell-by date."

Bob Willis on umpires

"Peter Siddle's heavy balls made life difficult."

Bob Willis

"If England lose, they'll be the losers."

Bob Willis

The funniest cricket broadcaster quotes!

"I guess some guys are just naturally built for comfort rather than cricket."

Bob Willis on Robert Key

"Steve Bucknor has completely lost the plot. He should take his pension back and sail off to the sunset."

Bob Willis

"That's what happens when, in cricketing parlance, the wheel comes off – and you can't steer the boat."

Bob Willis

THE FUNNIEST TENNIS QUOTES... EVER!

"You can not be serious!"

"I would take this f*****g ball and shove it down your f*****g throat."

www.ingramcontent.com/pod-product-compliance
Lightning Source LLC
Chambersburg PA
CBHW050303120526
44590CB00016B/2475